NEVER SAY I'M SORRY

NEVER SAY I'M SORRY

HOW TO AVOID REGRET

Samer G. Touma, Ph.D.

Charleston, SC
www.PalmettoPublishing.com

Never Say I'm Sorry
Copyright © 2021 by Samer G. Touma, Ph.D

First Edition

Hardcover ISBN: 978-1-63837-031-4
Paperback ISBN: 978-1-63837-032-1
eBook ISBN: 978-1-63837-033-8

To everyone whom I have ever encountered—thank you from the bottom my heart. This book is dedicated to you.

Always consider Spinoza's words "No matter how thin you slice it, there will always be two sides."

FOREWORD

As a child in Damascus, I spent a great deal of time with my grandmother. In the afternoons, when all the women in the family would converge on her home, they would share their thoughts and feelings about life. They often asked for each other's advice on issues of family, marriage, child rearing and on navigating friendships and life in general. This was life in the old world, the birthplace of civilization, where family and faith were the nucleus of everyday life.

During those times, I listened quietly and observed their interactions, what mattered most to them, and most importantly, how they solved the issues that inevitably arose in all relationships. Looking back, I believe that those times gave me the real-life fundamentals and the foundation I needed to become a therapist. I never really knew how much listening and observing influenced me—until much later. At 17 I drew a line across the globe and landed in Columbia South Carolina because of a favorable climate. I arrived speaking no English. I learned to read write and speak English by joining the English Program for Internationals at the University of South Carolina. I completed my Bachelor of Arts degree in International Studies and eventually pursued a master's degree in international affairs. Foreign policy and how the world falls apart or works together fascinated me; however, there were no employment opportunities in the field of international relations in South Carolina. After working in state government in career development for six years, I went back to school and enrolled to get my PhD. Since my master's degree was in international affairs, I was informed by the graduate program in educational psychology that I did not meet the criteria for admission into their doctorate program. Despite this challenge, I had a strong will and determination, and an underlying feeling that it was my vocation. I pursued the course work with a voracious appetite and was accepted into the program. I wrote my dissertation in roughly 6 months while raising three children and working three jobs. After completing my doctorate, I began my practice counseling children, adolescents, adults, and families. I'm grateful every day of my life for the privilege of being a counselor and therapist. My clients have taught me much about the power of the human spirit, about the potential in each of us, and, most importantly, about character. When we take time to develop insight into our own inner universe and accept who we are, we can begin to lay the foundation for our own character.

My journey as a therapist has taught me many things about life and people. It has expanded my universe and nurtured my soul. I have grown as a person. My own failures and transgressions have been the ladder to my redemption. My spirit is awakened with every therapeutic relationship. Most often, therapy is needed in times of crisis. People do not come to me when they are happy, but rather when they are going through a hardship. Yet, therapy is never about one thing; it can be about attachment, love, history, sorrow, learning, growth, disagreement, pain, confusion, being stuck, or being connected. The relationship between a therapist and a client is deeply intimate and one without judgment. As a therapist, my only goal is for my clients to speak their truth freely, because the truth will set them free.

My practice has also taught me about love, self-worth, children, marriage, divorce, professional commitment, spirituality, education, grief, friendship, forgiveness, relationships, success, and failure, as well as the importance of living a fulfilling life.

Some of the most difficult and profound questions I come across on a daily basis relate to life: What is the meaning of life? Is life worth living? How do I live a life that is worth living?

My encounters with the clients who had considered or attempted suicide have given me a glimpse of the answer. As I navigate life's journeys with them, the answer becomes more apparent each time.

Yes, life is worth living! Each day is a gift! When one is filled with regret, it is hard to see the possibility of anything beyond that feeling. Regret is a heavy burden. Most often, regret is something deep and unresolved in our psyche. Yes, most of us have regrets, but they do not have to weigh us down. They can be used as a springboard to achieve something greater and more satisfying than we could ever imagine. I was taught in my doctoral studies to observe and listen ninety percent of the time and work ten percent of the time. While working for this ten percent, I realized that I had much to offer my clients: love, acceptance, understanding, encouragement, a feeling of being valued, concern, a sense of perseverance, and—I think, most importantly—a pathway for investigating and examining their own behaviors, minds, souls, and spirits to find their answers. When my clients discovered and articulated the root of their regret, they learned to acknowledge, accept, and embrace what they have done. The acceptance helped them to learn from their mistakes and oversights and to use them as powerful tools to lay down the foundation for a good life. They began to develop character, integrity, and a real desire for the truth.

Within this book you will find many of my thoughts and opinions about our human journey. Over the years, the most important thing that I've requested most of my clients to keep in mind is gratitude. Please stop complaining. Life on earth is not heaven. It is not perfect. It is not meant to be perfect. It can often be very painful. However, it can also be fruitful, meaningful, and worth living. Life is a gift! Each one of us must find our own interpretations to understand our reality and live a meaningful life.

What has become most clear to me over all these years is those clients who have chosen to act with character are the ones who leave the crisis and my practice most successfully. First, I watch them go through the darkness of their life situation, and then I see them walk out of my office into the fullness of their lives, having overcome that darkness. Many times, I do not see them again, and wonder how they are doing. I often miss them.

Sometimes the clients have not behaved well in life. Frequently, they admit to having unintentionally compromised their integrity and character prior to entering therapy. During our time together, they are eventually faced with an important decision—perhaps the most important decision of their lives—to make a choice. They can choose to live with grace and good character or they can choose to live a vengeful and mean-spirited life. This is where they must do the work. All of us have this power of choice, yet so many people choose to play the role of a victim and believe that life has happened to them. These individuals take no responsibility for their actions.

They feel victimized and can never understand the single greatest concept.

Personal responsibility = freedom from regret

The simple act of recognizing that one always has a choice can inspire action and create a whole different view on life.

In this pursuit, some questions arise: How do you live a good life? What is needed for having fewer regrets? What is character?

I believe that you will find the answers to these questions in the pages that follow. Just as we teach our children the importance of "making good choices," my mission here is to assure you that it is never too late for YOU to make good choices, too, so you can develop good character and build a rich and fulfilling life, without regret.

A NOTE FROM THE AUTHOR

My mistakes, my transgressions, and the pain I have caused to others and to myself are my greatest teachers. Acknowledging and accepting them has played a large part in the process of developing my own character.

I regret hurting and causing harm to others and to myself. My mistakes and transgressions were the ladder to my redemption; understanding them laid the foundation on which I could build my own character.

To all the people who loved and supported me throughout my life—you've shown me the other side of life, one without regret. Most of you have accompanied me in my darkest moments. You've taught me how to build character, how to redeem myself, how to overcome and outgrow my flaws, and how to be a better person.

I am a better person because of you!
Thank you.

CONTENTS

CHARACTER

What is this notion of character? Character is perhaps the most important quality a person can possess. We know that character should be good and that it is valuable, but are we born with good character? No, we develop it. Let me say this again:

We are not born with good character—we develop it.

When we say someone is of good character, it is a constellation of their experiences and what they make of them. The components that influence good character include family, primary caregivers, extended family, acquaintances, friends, school, other adults, colleagues, and classmates as well as one's own failures and successes, and their observations of others.

The phrase "a person of character" sounds good when we say it, and we know that good character is valuable, but it remains a concept until we break it down into a practical, more pragmatic sense. Character is perhaps the most important quality in a person. It defines each and every one of us. The components of character are: respect, forgiveness, honor, gratefulness, and grace. Strength of character is not only about having these qualities but also about implementing them to exercise self-control and to resist temptation. To strengthen one's character is to mold oneself into a productive person. No doubt that it is ultimately about our personal choices, but when we act with character, we create a more peaceful and unbiased life that allows us to accept our human condition. By embracing it within ourselves, we naturally embrace it in others. We give people permission to be just as they are.

Strength of character is important for the following reasons:

- It allows us to carry out our will freely and enables us to cope with our setbacks. Thus, it helps us to reach our goals.
- It allows us to inquire into the causes of ill fortune instead of complaining about them.
- It gives us the perspective to see where our personal responsibilities lie.
- It gives us the courage to admit our own faults, imperfections, and weaknesses.
- It gives us the strength to keep a foothold when the tide turns against us and to continue to climb upward, overcoming all obstacles.
- It helps us to accept our reality and that of others, without judgment.
- It prevents us from constantly comparing ourselves to others. Such comparison leads to a greater level of dissatisfaction. Given the condition or situation of our life, we only compare ourselves to a small number of people, not the whole group of individuals. When this occurs, our dissatisfaction boomerangs and hits us in the face. For example, when comparing wealth, we naturally compare ourselves to rich people, and we feel very dissatisfied. However, if we were to compare ourselves with the poor, our dissatisfaction would be much lower. It is important to look at the whole spectrum, not just the upper end.

Character is a pattern of behaviors, thoughts, and feelings based on universal principles of moral strength and integrity— plus the courage to live by those principles every day. Character shows up in our life's virtues. It is the drive to do our best to avoid crossing the line, and it is the only thing that will help us get back on the good side of that line. It is our most valuable attribute that no one can ever take away. I have been labeled as brutally honest. I have spoken the truth to all varieties of people in my life—those I love, those I work with, and those I may never see again. We've heard the expression "the truth hurts;" however, it is that very truth that we need to hear, to say, and to believe to live a life of character. That is why character is important. It compels people to believe in us. It creates respect. Would you rather someone like you or respect you?

Integrity means adhering to a moral code of honesty, courage, strength, and truthfulness and being true to our word— even when no one is looking. As Don Miguel Ruiz writes in *The Four Agreements*, "Be impeccable with your word." When we are not true to our word, we lack integrity, and that's when we hurt others and ultimately ourselves the most.

When we cheat, our success is false. When we break a promise, we show that our word is meaningless. When we lie, we deceive others and lose their respect. These things can destroy our reputation and break the trust others have in us. Without good reputation and trustworthiness, our relationships fail. Relationships are the foundation for success in life. It is essential for an individual and for our collective society that we function together successfully. Each person must do his or her part every day by living with integrity.

When a student promises not to cheat but then does so, he/she is taking unfair advantage by putting himself ahead of others. He/she will ruin his/her reputation, academic record, and, potentially, job prospects.

When a businessman makes promises to his customers and doesn't deliver, he destroys his relationships with those customers. Ultimately, they go elsewhere, and his business fails.

When we destroy relationships with our friends, we feel isolated and lonely. By breaking our relationships, we pollute the foundation for success in our life. We need each other to survive.

Who is more successful? Someone who is famous and makes a great deal of money, or someone who has no fame, makes little money, but is, for example, a great parent? Are we placing too much value on net worth, prestige, a big house, and a high-paying job? Are we putting too much emphasis on good grades and high test scores in schools today? Do these things really define our success?

What do we value? Is it money, power, and fame at any cost? Or, is it good character by showing respect for others, offering forgiveness, having honor, being grateful, and showing grace for all mankind?

You decide.

It really is up to you.

In the following pages, I will discuss what I define as aspects of good character. As you read, I ask that you contemplate the possibilities and maybe, just maybe, apply some of the ideas to your own life. Let's see if my humble opinion can help you gain insight and begin your journey to a satisfying and meaningful life. Most importantly, you may be able to never say I'm Sorry.

RESPECT

If they respect you, respect them. If they disrespect you, still respect them. Do not allow the actions of others to decrease your good manners, because you represent yourself, not others.
~Zeyara

Respecting your boundaries guarantees respecting the boundaries of others. ~Remas

RESPECT

The word "respect" fascinates me. It is one of the many words that we often use without understanding their meanings. It can be defined as admiration for oneself or others that elicits positive feelings. Respect for ourselves means doing away with negative self-talk and embracing ourselves as we are—right here and now. It is a major component of character. Without self-respect and respect for others, nothing in our world would be able to function, because people will trample on each other's freedom. This will lead to chaos.

We often mistake respect for agreement. We can respect thunder, but not agree with it. Respect is the ability to understand, accept, and embrace a person, a group, an idea, or nature when we don't agree with it. Respect means behaving in a manner that is embracing and accepting without an aggressive response. We can agree. We can disagree. We can do either one in a way that is comfortable and reasonable without having to react violently. Without respect, however, disagreements become destructive. If we don't respect nature, we destroy it. If we don't respect others, we reject them. If we don't respect ourselves, we defile and desecrate ourselves. We forget that our body is our temple. We abuse ourselves and just because our body does not react immediately it doesn't mean that it will not eventually let us know. If we don't respect ideas, we regress and don't become enlightened. Respect is necessary for us to live and thrive in a civilized, mindful world. The root of most problems, troubles, and issues, whether personal or cultural, is a lack of respect.

How do we earn respect? How do we offer it? The answer to both questions requires living responsibly, using our own natural energy, having a spiritual component in our lives, developing a set of personal ethics, striving for excellence, and being tolerant and thoughtful. How do we do this? By trying to understand the subcomponents of "respect."

R.E.S.P.E.C.T.

- **Responsibility**

  Responsibility is commitment. It means following through and doing what we say we are going to do. Many of us say things without following through. This makes us lose credibility in the eyes of others. When we fail to follow through often enough, then we lose our self-respect. We get down on ourselves, end up swimming in our own heads, and begin to waste precious time and energy in doubting ourselves. When we doubt ourselves, other people can feel it, and they, too, begin to doubt us; hence, we lose more credibility. To stop this downward spiral, we must not make false promises or fail to keep our word. Responsibility within ourselves leads to credibility with others.

- **Energy**

  Have you ever started something and not finished it? How did that feel? Did it impact other people in your life? How did they feel about it? Were you able to have a frank and open conversion about it? I believe one of the reasons we may leave something unfinished is that we don't have enough motivation or emotional energy to stay the course.

When we are not able to finish what we start, we lose respect for ourselves. We feel like a failure, and sometimes we end up running away and hiding from the truth. When we involve friends, family, and colleagues in our endeavors that we leave unfinished, then all these people begin to lose respect for us as well. Why do we do this? I believe that one of the reasons for leaving something unfinished is that we don't have enough motivation or emotional energy to stay on the course. Our lives are just too cluttered and our priorities are off-kilter. We allow ourselves to get involved in too many things that pull us in multiple directions, and finally we are not left with enough time to follow through. One effective way to maintain our energy is to have clear priorities, to have less to do, and to follow through with our commitments. When we commit to our priorities and get things done, people will naturally respect us. And we in turn will we have more energy. Another reason that drains our energy is anxiety. We often generate anxiety on our own, especially when we make assumptions without any clarification. When we make assumptions, everything around us becomes personal and we take it to heart in negative ways. For example, when someone doesn't respond to our text or call, we might assume that they don't like us or are angry with us - assumptions that may be inaccurate. We can slide down the slippery slope of negative emotions and start feeling bad about ourselves and others—all based on an assumption made without any clarification. However, there is a difference between emotions and feelings. We are actually born with a set of emotions such as fear, love, excitement, and sorrow. Various reactions from our environment to our emotions shape and develop our feelings. Emotions are energy. Both movement and behavior are energy driven; therefore, our emotions affect our energy.

- **Spirituality**

  Spirituality is not about a particular religion or God, it is universal. I believe that spirituality is about recognizing and believing that there is something bigger than ourselves. It is about a sense of morality and truth in general. Spirituality always involves giving and being self-aware. When we give of ourselves, we are in a perfect state of existence. When we give, we feel good deep down inside. However, there is one challenge to this: we cannot give without knowing what we have to give. Spirituality gives us peace of mind to figure out that part. Spirituality is a value and belief system that recognizes what is right and what is wrong. Simply put, spirituality is a connection to truth. When we are spiritual, we offer ourselves for service and give our time and talent naturally, selflessly, and purely. Part of being spiritual is knowing the essence of our existence. It is about respecting our soul, our value system, and our belief system. When we are in touch with our own moral code, we truly feel our connection to society and to each other. When others can see us in our best light, they develop respect for us. When we violate that which connects our core to society, we lose respect for ourselves. In turn, others don't see us in our best light.

- **Personal ethics**

  Personal ethics implies a personal belief system. It is being accountable for what we do. Do I hold myself accountable? When I do something that violates another person, another culture, or the law, do I acknowledge it and learn from it? Or do I convince myself that what I did is okay? The phrase "never waste a mistake" means we must hold ourselves accountable and learn from our experiences. We need to take ownership of our mistakes and make a conscious effort not to repeat them. It's been said "Good judgment comes from experience, which is mostly full of bad judgment." It is imperative to leave our own defensiveness at the door and not justify our behavior. We need to acknowledge our mistakes, accept them, and take responsibility for them. When we accept our flaws and transgressions, we connect with our humanity, and then we can finally begin to gain respect for ourselves and others.

- **Excellence**

  Excellence doesn't mean we have to be the best, but it does mean that we strive to do our best. We must use and share our talents and gifts to the best of our ability. This is one of our most basic human responsibilities. Excellence leads to self-respect and fosters the respect from others. The path to excellence involves valuing what we are good at, having a moral code to which we hold ourselves accountable, and having a strong work ethic. Work should not only be about making money but also about knowing what we can achieve personally and professionally and then following through on it.

Excellence does not mean that we never fail. It means that we see and accept our mistakes, and then we correct them, thus becoming a better person. Nothing should stop us from pursuing excellence and doing our best, otherwise we rob ourselves and others of our gifts. The concept of excellence applies to all aspects of our social lives—relationships, marriages, friendships, etc. Excellence is needed to be a good, honest friend or parent. Excellence also includes keeping our word. If we say we are going to do something, we are obliged to finish it. Our word is our bond.

- **Care**
  We must learn to care for ourselves before we can care for others. By nurturing ourselves spiritually, physically, mentally, and emotionally, we enhance our ability to nurture others. We need to slow down and listen to ourselves and others in this journey of caring. Caring starts with politeness, for example, it may be as simple as saying hello and goodbye to people. Caring for something doesn't mean that it should be limited to thoughts only, it is an action, a verb. Caring for others means being thoughtful about their condition. We must be mindful of how we fit into another person's world and how we influence and impact it. Caring is a constant and consistent action of tending to others. There are many ways to care such as caring for people in need, caring about our spiritual growth, actively seeking the truth, and last but not least caring about our environment. Caring means that we do not destroy or contribute to the demise of anyone or anything. These

ways of caring are the building blocks of healthy and meaningful relationships.

- **Tolerance and thoughtfulness**

  Do we tolerate the opinions and tastes of others, or have we created a judgmental culture? Is it possible for us to be tolerant of others, or are we an intolerant species? It is crucial that we remain careful not to impose our personal moral code on other people. Our moral code is ours alone, and no one else's, for they may have a different one. It is important not to judge or discount the opinions of others. It is okay to have differing opinions and still accept others for who they are, rather than who we want them to be. Marriages that have withstood the test of time are the ones where the partners are tolerant of each other. It is important to have complete acceptance of others in order to let them bloom and blossom. When we are tolerant of someone for who they are, we show respect for them and for ourselves, because we accept that they are simply human, and, by extension, so are we. By being tolerant of ourselves, we let our authentic selves shine through, and give others permission to do the same. Tolerance does not mean agreement, rather it means accepting people for who they are. We accept the flower when it blooms, so why not give that to other people? Intolerance leads to aggression and it can harm us and others. Thoughtfulness is giving our mind the opportunity to see the world through other people's perspectives, not those of our own. It allows us to consider multiple points of view on a situation, which again means accepting what is and embracing what needs to be done in order to improve our life and the lives of those around us. Another form of this is mindfulness, which is the ability to walk through other people's lives carefully and with an awareness of what causes harm, to us or to others, and to actively avoid that harm. Mindfulness is allowing things to be as they are, not as we want them to be. In this way we can avoid self-centeredness and self-absorption, and we can see the world through a wider, more considerate, and more thoughtful lens. All this is part of tolerance.

When we implement the qualities of R.E.S.P.E.C.T. in our lives, we show respect for ourselves and others. So, why is respect important? What is the goal here? The answers to these questions are:

1. To have a life worth living.
2. To coexist harmoniously with ourselves, with other people, and with everything all around us.
3. To feel good about our existence.
4. To give something to the world around us.
5. To extract as much as we can from the world around us.

If we choose not to be respectful, we are choosing to live in a chaotic world, both internally and externally. We can't survive, let alone thrive, or even maintain a status quo, in such chaos. When we are respectful, we live a life worth living.

FORGIVE

I never knew how strong I was until I had to forgive someone
who wasn't sorry and accept an apology I never received.
~Anonymous

Forgiveness is unlocking the door to set someone free and realizing
you were the prisoner.
~Max Lucado

In the blink of an eye everything can change. So, forgive often and
love with all your heart. You may not have that chance again.
~Zig Ziglar

FORGIVE

When someone we care about hurts us, we can hold on to anger, resentment, and thoughts of revenge—or, we can embrace forgiveness and move forward. Sounds easy, right? Not at all. We have all been hurt by someone, either by someone we know and love or by strangers, or perhaps by both. Perhaps our mother criticized our parenting skills, our colleague sabotaged a project, or our partner abandoned us. These wounds can leave us with lasting feelings of anger, bitterness, and even vengeance; however, if we don't practice forgiveness, we might be the one who pays most dearly.

Those who have gone through the divorce process know this as well as anyone. When we choose to forgive, we are also choosing peace, hope, gratitude, and joy over negative emotions. Forgiveness can lead us to physical, emotional, and spiritual well-being.

What is forgiveness? Put simply, it is letting go of resentment and thoughts of revenge. The act of someone that hurt or offended us might remain a part of our life forever, but forgiveness can lessen its grip on us and allow us to focus on the positive parts of our life. Forgiveness often leads to understanding, empathy, and compassion for the one who has hurt us.

Forgiveness doesn't mean that we stop holding a person responsible for hurting us, and it doesn't minimize or justify the wrongdoing. We can forgive the person without excusing the act. Forgiveness gives us the peace that helps us go on with life.

Letting go of grudges and bitterness can make way for compassion, kindness, and peace. Letting go is a form of surrender that can lead to the following:

- Healthier relationships;
- Greater spiritual and psychological well-being;
- Less anxiety, stress, and hostility;
- Lower blood pressure;
- Fewer symptoms of depression; and
- Lower risk of alcohol and substance abuse.

When someone we love or trust hurts us, we might feel angry, sad, or confused. In fact, we can feel any combination of the many negative emotions. If we dwell on hurtful events or situations or hold grudges filled with resentment, then feelings of vengeance and hostility can take root. If we allow negative feelings to fester and crowd out positive feelings, we will find ourselves swallowed up by our own bitterness or sense of injustice.

If we're unforgiving, we might pay the price again and again by bringing anger and bitterness into every relationship and new experience. Our life might become so wrapped up in the wrong that we won't be able to enjoy the present moment. We might become depressed or anxious. We might feel that our life lacks meaning or purpose, or that we're at odds with our spiritual beliefs. We might lose valuable and enriching connections with others.

Forgiveness is an active process that involves fulfillment, seizing the opportunity, repairing connections, generating energy, being intentional in our thoughts and actions, living by our virtue, and eventually entering into a wholesome new way of being.

F.O.R.G.I.V.E.

- **Fulfillment**

  Do you know what fulfillment really means? It means experiencing satisfaction and joy as a result of fully developing one's abilities or character. An often overlooked way to feel fulfilled is through the act of forgiving others. Forgiving is for us, not for anyone else. It allows us to achieve a sense of satisfaction, which helps us feel complete and whole. When we withhold forgiveness, we create an empty spot in our mind and in our soul. This empty space prevents us from the freedom of feeling fulfilled. Fulfillment is about being content; it doesn't mean anything more. When we are at peace with our current situation, we feel fulfilled, whole, and complete. When we finish a good meal, we feel full and then we stop. We tend to have an obsession with more in our culture. Fulfillment is about recognizing that we are full and knowing when enough is enough. Oftentimes we just don't know when to stop.

- **Opportunity**

  Life is full of opportunities to forgive and to be for-
  given. These opportunities are all around us, available
  all the time, every day. We must seize each and every
  opportunity to forgive. For example, an opportunity
  may present itself when we get cut off in traffic, when
  we are in a grocery store, at home, at school, in court,
  in church—at any place. We find opportunities to
  live meaningful lives, to start over, and to rejuvenate
  throughout the daily process of living. Why not take
  the time to slow down and experience forgiveness? It
  is up to us to recognize and make the most of these
  opportunities wherever we find them.

- **Repair**

  One of the most important aspects of forgiving is repair.
  It means remaining open to the other party and giving
  them space to approach us, to take responsibility for
  their actions and bad behavior, and to apologize. Repair
  is listening to see if others have truly realized that they
  have hurt us, and are able to empathize with us, for if
  they do—all we need to do in return is to reach deep
  down into our own humanity and simply say thank you.
  How can we give someone who has hurt us an opportunity to repair the damage? Why must we? Because while
  it is their job to work on the repair, we can assist them by
  demonstrating good character and helping them along
  in the process. We can pave the road for them to feel
  comfortable in this process of repair by being open to
  their overtures. We can be approachable, but sometimes
  we can't stop there, as the process may require us to reach

out to others to bring them to the table to do this work. We may even need to join them.

- **Generating energy**
  Forgiveness gives us energy and helps us generate new energy—freedom! Freedom frees up our minds from the heavy burden of suffering that occurs when we are angry and unforgiving. When we stop the incessant loop of anger in our heads, we generate energy that frees us from the heaviness of not letting go. Forgiveness allows us to feel our vitality and strengthens the natural regenerative life force inside us. Hence, we are able to create space for new opportunities and to make genuine connections in all areas of our lives.

- **Intent**
  Forgiveness is an intentional way of living. It cannot occur unless we choose it. It is a choice that needs to be made constantly, on a daily basis. Would we rather like to be a person who holds onto the grudges and pain, and relives all of those dark scenarios? Or, would we rather be a forgiving person, and be free of the burden? We must focus on making a choice to forgive and not allow the past to penetrate the present, for when it does, it contaminates the purity of our heart. It takes daily work to stay focused on the present state of being forgiving.

- **Virtue**
  Forgiveness is our moral obligation; it is a virtue to maintain civility and avoid hostility. The ability to forgive is an admirable virtue that promotes strength and

power within us. Being virtuous means that we abide by a strong moral code. By being virtuous, we bring goodness and righteousness into our world and share it with the people around us. To be virtuous is to recognize and embrace our moral code, to understand it, and, finally, to implement it.

For example, if my moral code prohibits gossip, but I find myself participating in gossip, how do I stop? First, I must recognize that I am gossiping. Second, I must consciously and actively understand why gossiping is bad—the pros and cons. Finally, I must actively stop gossiping, thus implementing my virtue by putting my values into action.

- **Entrance**
Life is all about growth. Without growth we die. When we forgive, we can grow, flourish, and blossom. This allows us to enter a new realm of existence where we may find a new level of joy, fresh opportunities, and new relationships. We have so many opportunities to grow, but how can we grow if we hold grudges? When we live in a state of forgiveness, each day brings about new opportunities to enter the world of another, with empathy and compassion. We must allow all of our senses to enter when we come into the heart of a new domain, a new idea, or a new perspective. It is important that as we enter we allow it to be, even though sometimes it can be highly unpleasant. Entrance allows us to be at peace with the universe. Think of other people as nature. We watch and allow thunder, storms, flowers,

and sunshine, and we do not allow it to consume us. Can we do this for other human beings?

Forgiveness means accepting a wrongdoing and choosing not to react to it in a negative way. It's about accepting that a hurtful incident has occurred and choosing not to allow it to contaminate our existence, that is, our everyday life and the way we function. We must practice forgiveness in all domains of life, and not allow others or their behavior to change us.

HONOR

If you hear that someone is speaking ill of you, instead of trying to defend yourself you should say: "He obviously does not know me very well, since there are so many other faults he could have mentioned."
~Epictetus

Always try to be nice, but never fail to be kind.
~Anonymous

Out of suffering have emerged the strongest souls; the most massive characters are seared with scars.
~Khalil Gibran

HONOR

Honor is honesty, fairness, and integrity in one's beliefs and actions. When we have honor, we offer hope, openness, nobility, obligation, and rank to others and ourselves.

H.O.N.O.R.

- **Hope**
  Remember the movie *The Shawshank Redemption*? My favorite quote from that movie goes something like this: "Hope is a good thing, maybe the best of things, and no good thing ever dies." Such a true statement! Most often, we hope for better things out of life. We honor life the most when we keep our hopes alive. It is hope that keeps us moving forward. Believing in someone is the same as having hope for them. It is the unbiased, genuine desire for the other to have options and to allow them the freedom to exercise those options. Hope is a positive, creative choice that helps us to be better, not bitter. Time flows forward, not backward and hope is a forward-moving process. There is no future without hope. Having hope means embracing life's ever-changing ways, while constantly believing that the best is yet to come.

- **Openness**
  Openness means being in a judgment-free zone and respecting and moving gently through the world around us. We need to be open to cultures, ideas, and ways of

living that are different from our own. When we are open, it allows us to honor not only ourselves but also the diverse world in which we live. Openness is about becoming transparent and letting the world know who we truly are, without imposing our beliefs on others. Furthermore, it is the ability to accept different points of view from others regardless of whether we agree or disagree with them.

- **Nobility**

  Nobility means having moral excellence and looking at another human being with genuine care, and simply put, plain old common decency. My mother-in-law says, "Times may change, but decency remains the same." Nobility is the way we conduct ourselves, and it shows in our character and dignity. It is important to reflect on how we treat others and ourselves despite social demands and fads. Difficult times in our lives offer us opportunities to handle situations with nobility and character. We honor others by acting with nobility. When we treat others with decency, nobility, and genuine care, we offer them the space to be themselves, without imposing any of our preconceived ideas on them.

- **Obligation**

  An important part of honoring ourselves and our self-respect is recognizing what we should do, and do-ing it. It is about understanding what needs to be fa-cilitated, and facilitating it. It is knowing what's neces-sary, and then meeting the necessity. However, most of us struggle between what we want to do and what we ought to do. We all have obligations. When we neglect them, we act dishonorably; however, when we meet them, it contributes to our satisfaction and makes us feel a sense of oneness with the world. People generally have a negative connotation about obligation because it's something that one ought to do, and not what one wants to do. This is a misinterpretation. Obligation is instead an act of love. When we meet our obligations, we feel accomplished. We feel a sense of wholeness and completeness. Eventually, it makes us feel good about our existence. It is a known fact that when we meet our goals and obligations, our brain produces more serotonin—a neurohormone that makes us feel joyful and mentally and psychologically satisfied.

- **Rank**

  By rank here, I mean priorities. When we have our priorities in order, we know what needs to be done, and we do it! Rank is our ability to understand our priorities, determine their importance relative to everything else in our lives, list them in order, and get them done. We often neglect our priorities, get fixated on less significant things, and just drop the ball. This happens when we get overwhelmed, sidelined, sidetracked, or allow our own compulsions to supersede our responsibilities. When important things pile up and we neglect them, we behave inappropriately. We must do those things first that are given highest rank on our list of priorities so that we feel we are being true to ourselves and to those whose lives may be impacted by our actions, or inactions.

We need to be constantly and consistently mindful and aware of our priorities, values, and principles. It is an active part of our existence. Most of us act honorably, but we don't recognize it as such. For example, when I tell someone that they are an honorable person or have performed an honorable act, they give me a bewildered look, as if what they did doesn't measure up to their idea of honorable. It's important to note that most people behave in an honorable way, but instead of embracing such behavior as honorable, we look at honor as something unachievable and rare. The more we think of our actions as honorable, the more inspired and motivated we are to continue to behave honorably.

GRATITUDE

Gratitude is not only the greatest of virtues, but the parent of all the others. ~Marcus Tullius

When you arise in the morning, think of what a precious privilege it is to be alive; to breathe, to think, to enjoy, to love. ~Marcus Aurelius

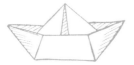

GRATEFUL

Being grateful is expressing appreciation for what we have—as opposed to a consumer-oriented emphasis on what we want or need. Gratitude adds to our general well-being. Studies show that when we deliberately cultivate gratitude, we contribute positively to our well-being and happiness. Also, grateful thinking—and especially expressing it to others—is associated with increased levels of energy, optimism, and empathy. Living with gratitude is a major component of a character driven life.

G.R.A.T.E.F.U.L.

- **Gentleness**
  We live hectic lives, cluttered with too many commitments, thoughts, and feelings. Our lives are not easily or comfortably managed. We often find ourselves overwhelmed, and then we become harsh with ourselves and everyone around us. If we find ourselves losing patience easily, it is a sure sign that it's time to slow down and take stock. Which areas of our lives are most important to us? Where can we cut back? What can we do to stop negativity, including negative self-talk? How can we be gentler with ourselves? Being gentle with ourselves and others is one of the most important aspects of being kind and grateful.

- **Reflection**
  It is important to reflect and remember. Not simply on the bad things and those who wronged us, but also on all of the things that have enriched our lives. Can you sit back and recall some of the small wonders that have graced your life? We need to focus on simple things, like a kind act from someone, good weather, the ability

to work, or the fact that we are healthy. Remembering and reflecting on goodness, kindness, blessings, and gifts, regardless of how big or small, will enhance our lives. When we take the time to do this daily, it becomes a habit. Once it has become a habitual way of thinking and acting, we then have the opportunity to share this way of being with others in our lives. When we share it, our individual light can spark a thousand other lights. Expressing our gratitude can make more people feel the beauty of being grateful.

- **Attitude**

   Attitude is the way we conduct ourselves and interact with others. Attitude is how we express our belief system toward the outer world. It is our inner perception and perspective of the world around us and how we display and show ourselves to others. Our attitude shows not only in our words but also in our body language, our state of mind, and our personal energy. When we are grateful, it shows in our body, our language, and even on our face. A grateful soul has a bright sheen to their being. A disposition of kindness and softness that communicates much more than the spoken word. Having a pleasant, open attitude displays a tremendous level of gratitude. Do we approach the world with appreciation and acceptance, or with judgment and rejection? If we believe that individuals in a social setting are judgmental, our attitude will show up in the skeptical way we approach them and present ourselves to them. If we believe that the social group is accepting of us, it will show up as increased confidence. When we believe that the world is a good place to be in, it brings the attitude of gratitude and appreciation to the fore. If we assume that the world is a difficult place, we show rejection, judgment, displeasure, dissatisfaction, and unpleasantness in our attitude. Whether positive or negative, our attitude is noticeable and glaring in our interactions with others.

- **Temptation**

  Human beings are created to maintain themselves and survive. Temptation shows up when we least expect it, often when we feel weak and vulnerable. It arrives when our egos need some stroking and when we have put our own needs above all else. This desire is normal, but it can lead to our downfall. What we don't see in those moments is that our burning needs are precisely what we must resist, because it can and often will cause harm. We tend to focus on what we don't have instead of what we do have. However, it is imperative that we resist the temptation of our ego and its arrogance. The path of temptation is driven by self-centeredness and selfishness, and when we allow ourselves to go down that path, we ignore others' needs. We end up stepping on other people's toes to get what we want. We harm others on our way to satisfy our desires. Temptation has no positive attributes. It only leads to destruction; however, being able to control our temptation and desires leads to better emotional and behavioral self-management and regulation. We can create an equilibrium in which we secure our needs, but not at the expense of others' needs. We all have the strength within us to say no to temptation. And when we do so, we find ourselves back in the world of gratitude and there we are at ease.

- **Elicit**

  Only feeling grateful is not enough. We must convey the idea of being grateful in our words, thoughts, and actions. We must elicit a state of gratitude in our daily life to evoke the good in everything around us. How many times have we felt grateful toward someone and not told them? How often do we say a kind word to someone about a certain friend, but never directly to that friend? Many times we feel grateful toward others, but we do not show it or let them know it directly. How many times have we waited until it was too late to show our gratitude for someone? There are so many ways to elicit the feelings and actions of gratitude. Can we think of some of the ways that can spread the goodness of gratitude? It is important to draw out meaningful ways to express our gratitude.

- **Fear**

  Fear is the supreme emotion. It can keep us alive and well in some situations, but fear can also prevent us from being grateful by pushing us to hold onto things that we don't need. We can accumulate any number of things that clutter our lives. Fear keeps us on the path of acquiring as much as we can, even more than we need. When the supply is more than demand, then the value of the supply decreases. Similarly, acquiring too much stops us from being grateful for all the good things in our lives. Fear can also keep us from being open to new ideas, new opportunities, or new relationships. It holds us back from a more positive life. When we become paralyzed with fear, we forget everything and remain stuck in our heads and closed off from our own lives. Hence, overcoming fear is very important.

- **Unity**
  It is important to recognize that we are all part of the puzzle of life. We are connected to everything around us, whether we want to be or not is of no consequence. We should recognize the unity we have with all parts of the world. Several years ago, my wife and I visited the Redwood National Park in California. I was overwhelmed with a feeling of reverence for all of life. The trees were hundreds of years old, and I was only a fraction of their age. I would never be able to estimate or know what they had seen and experienced! I could not bring myself to even touch one of them. I felt that I was a part of something so much bigger, older, and wiser. I felt unity in my bones. Our lives are like the inside of a kaleidoscope; all of the pieces connect and unite to form a picture. When one piece moves, the whole picture changes. Being mindful of this unity and connectedness gives us a sense of gratitude for the whole picture.

- **Love**
  The most important part of gratitude is love—for all living things, for nature, and for a higher being. We

need to do more than simply tell people that we love them. We need to act in a loving way. We need to demonstrate our love through our actions because that is when gratitude becomes real. To love is to feel, experience, act, and contribute. Love comes in many forms and dimensions. To be grateful is to give love and know how to receive it. Love is not just a noun, it is a verb. It is being empathetic, understanding, accepting, genuine, sincere, and without judgment. Love is embracing the world around us with all its differences and allowing ourselves and others to exist in harmony. Love is the antithesis of selfishness and self-centeredness. Love is appreciation; it is giving even when we don't receive. Love is non-transactional and unconditional. Love is a one-way street.

As we can see, being grateful is not simply saying "thank you" or "I appreciate it." Being grateful encompasses a multidimensional way of living. It is a way of being. When we are grateful it radiates all around us.

GRACE

KINDNESS is the language which the deaf can hear and the blind can see.
~Mark Twain

For beautiful eyes, look for the good in others; for beautiful lips, speak only words of kindness; and for poise, walk with the knowledge that you are never alone.
~Audrey Hepburn

GRACE

Grace is a spiritual way of living where we do not disturb what is around us, whether its nature or people. It's about walking through life without rummaging through it. It's about smelling the flower without having to pluck it, because if we do, it will eventually die. We can live gracefully, and we can die gracefully. Grace is the beginning and the end.

G.R.A.C.E.

- **Giving**

    Something wonderful happens to us when we give. Our minds and souls are in a perfect state of existence. The one who gives often receives as much joy as the recipient. Giving to others infuses us with life. Sharing time, talents, and treasures with other people makes them feel special. Simple acts like smiling or holding the door for a stranger can make that person feel valued. We can give big lavish gifts for holidays and birthdays, and we can also give small tokens of gratitude through our words and actions every day. Even sending kind thoughts to others silently is a form of giving. The key here is to always give. To give when we don't feel like it. To give when we are exhausted or have the least motivation to do so. The most important thing to remember is to give from our heart. When we do so, it will touch the other person's heart.

- **Rejuvenation**

    Each day we have the opportunity for a fresh start. We can choose to let go of old grievances and free ourselves from the past, or we can allow the past to drag us into that destructive downward spiral time and again. I believe the former is the best approach. Letting go of the past allows us to rejuvenate and continually renew our commitment to goodness. I am not saying forget the past—not at all! We cannot change unless we embrace the fullness of our shadow, that is, our own darkness and mistakes. The secret is to make that most important personal vow and do all that we can to never make those same mistakes again. Let each day be a chance to make things better by allowing the energy of good character to be our guide.

- **Action**
  Our thoughts and feelings, however good and strong, cannot do much without action. Let our good energy be a positive force in this world! If we feel love, we should say it, write it, sing it, show it, dance it, paint it in whatever way—but do it! Let others know how we feel today. Don't wait until one of us is sick, or even worse, at our funeral. If we owe someone an apology, we must swallow our pride and apologize. If we love someone, we must be vulnerable and say it, without the expectation that they will say it back to us. If we notice the kindness of others, lift them up by addressing them. It is amazing how powerful we can be when we put thoughts and feelings into action. We must not hide how we feel, we should let it show in our attitude, our body language, and our actions!

- **Connectedness**
  We can establish connections with people all around us. Simple things like greeting others, listening,

hugging, or holding hands can create long-lasting bonds. Connectedness is not only physical. Where appropriate, it is about observing the world around us and allowing our observations to sink in, to be understood by us and, if needed, to relate our observations to others for their benefit. Connectedness is about sharing and allowing others to share, about giving and being a gracious recipient, about believing and allowing ourselves to be believed, and about embracing ourselves and what we deserve and recognizing that others are just as deserving. It is important that we actually express these thoughts verbally and through our actions. When I give people feedback, I say "I am not giving you a compliment, I am just sharing my observations." If the feedback happens to be complimentary, then it is a compliment. If it's not complimentary, it's not criticism. Connectedness is about developing a mutual understanding and acceptance of what is going on. When we connect, we share our thoughts, our feelings, and ourselves with others and allow others to do the same.

- **Embracing reality**
  Sometimes embracing our reality instead of fighting it can make a big difference. We should stop wishing for a better life, embrace our giftedness, and work toward what we want. We should avoid ignoring our mistakes. If we know in our heart or feel in our gut that we have hurt someone, then we must address it. True character shines through when we take on the seemingly impossible, lean into our discomfort, and do what's right, no matter how exposed we might feel. It is important to

hold on to our mistakes gently, but only for as long as it takes to learn from them. Eventually we must let them go. By embracing reality, we help guide the direction of our destiny.

Grace is our ability and desire to display warmth, softness, elegance, beauty, generosity, helpfulness, goodwill, and mercy as we go through our day-to-day life. Grace is found in giving. It rejuvenates us and encourages us to take more positive actions. It helps us connect to others, and that, in turn, allows us to see and embrace reality on a larger scale.

CONCLUSION

Our good character is the most important asset we have. Character takes a lifetime to build, yet it can be lost in an instant. Once lost, it is difficult to regain. Our true character is revealed when no one else is looking. When we choose short-term gain or an easy fix to a problem, we may be doing the wrong thing. Consider the old adage, "We are what we do." This is a true statement. Failure to consider the long-term consequences of our actions can be not only dangerous but also disastrous. The danger comes when we jump on an impulse in a moment of temptation, without considering the impact it will have on others. I am talking about the collateral damage. Once the grenade is thrown, there is no turning back—and that is the disaster. It can be a simple hug, an innocent conversation, or a full-blown affair. It could be a little white lie because of our own discomfort. It could also be innocently hiding something hurtful. By focusing on the importance of character, we will be guided by principles, moral strength, and integrity to do the right thing. Nothing is more important for true success in our life than our good character.

The process presented in this text is based on what I have learned so far. Now it's yours - take it or leave it. These ideas have been generated by my own personal struggles, pain, trials, triumphs, and failures. I can't say that by doing this once in the morning, once at noon, and once at night you will have built your character. It's not that easy. But I promise you that this is all that's needed. How you choose to implement it is up to you. What I do know is this: When we truly live by these ideas, concepts, and notions, we will become a person of character. Eventually, we will live in peace with a greater sense of appreciation for life in every aspect, and we will have the ability to tackle life's painful and dark moments in a way that is more productive than destructive. Most importantly, you will live more proactively than reactively, and hence will feel more fulfilled and complete.

This is not a manifesto for life. It is just one way to look at it from my humble perspective as a husband, a father, a friend, and a counselor. I am sharing it with you because I believe that if we all took steps toward a life of character, the world would have much less pain. I see so much self-inflicted pain in my practice and all around me that I wish I had a magic wand, and I could take everyone's pain away. Sadly, I know this is not possible. What I do have, however, are the words in this book that have helped me live a better life. I still have pain, but it is far less than the quotient of peace in my heart. Building character is not like taking a magic pill. It is a daily process of holding ourselves accountable and accepting what the day brings. As difficult as it sometimes might be, it is important to make a conscious effort to have respect, develop forgiveness, create honor, express gratitude, and live with grace. These are the qualities that make up character. I believe that this is the foundation for a meaningful existence in this life.

ABOUT DR. SAMER TOUMA

Dr. Samer Touma earned his PhD in counseling from the Department of Educational Psychology, University of South Carolina. His major emphasis is on children, adolescents, and families.

Dr. Touma participated in post-doctoral specialized training at the University of South Carolina in advanced psychopathology and personality disorders (diagnosis and treatment) in children, adolescents, and adults. In addition, he has acquired advanced training in psychopathology testing and assessment for designation to assess and treat serious mental health problems.

He is a Board-Certified Forensic Mental Health Evaluator and a Board-Certified Child Custody Evaluator. Dr. Touma has been qualified to testify in court as an expert regarding a variety of mental health issues throughout South Carolina. In particular, he is qualified to testify as an expert in child custody, post-divorce issues, and parental capacity.

Dr. Touma has taught graduate-level courses at a number of universities in South Carolina. He founded the counseling program at Webster University – Columbia South Carolina and served as department chair for eleven years. He has served on the South Carolina licensing board for counselors from 2011 to 2015 at the appointment of the governor of South Carolina.